Pursuit

Pursuit

Poems by

Karen Neuberg

© 2019 Karen Neuberg. All rights reserved.
This material may not be reproduced in any form, published,
reprinted, recorded, performed, broadcast,
rewritten or redistributed without
the explicit permission of Karen Neuberg.
All such actions are strictly prohibited by law.

Cover design by Shay Culligan

ISBN: 978-1-950462-34-6

Kelsay Books Inc.

kelsaybooks.com

502 S 1040 E, A119
American Fork, Utah 84003

With love to my family—
Alan, Liz, Jesse, Gabe, and Seth

Acknowledgments

Grateful acknowledgment is made to the editors of the following publications in which some of these poems first appeared, sometimes in a slightly different form and/or with different titles:

*Barrow Street, The Broken City, Buffalo Carp, Caffeine Destiny, Caliban Online, Counterexample Poetics, decomP, Diner, The Dirty Napkin, elimae, Epigraph Magazine, erato, Hermeneutic Chaos Literary Journal, Home Planet News, JMWW, Lingerpost: A Literary Journal, Little River, Mannequin Envy, Marathon Literary Review, Menacing Hedge, Muddy River Poetry Review, Myself Taking Stage (*Finishing Line Press, 2014*), The Nassau Review, Oak Bend Review, Otoliths, Paper Nautilus, phoebe, Pirene's Fountain 10th Anniversary Issue, The Poetry Distillery, Poetrybay, {Prong & Posy}, Really System, Red Eft Review, Right Hand Pointing, The Same, Serving House Journal, Shot Glass Journal, Silver Stork, Storm Cellar, Southern Florida Poetry Journal (SoFloPoJo), Superstition Review, Tinderbox Poetry Journal, tinfoildresses, Toasted Cheese Literary Journal, TXTOBJX, Unbroken Journal, Wazee Journal, Words on Paper Literary Review, and Zingara Poetry Review.*

My thanks and gratitude to the writers and artists whose creativity and generosity continue to inspire me. Especially Catherine Arra, Amy Barone, Patricia Carragon, Kelly Cressio-Moeller, Bob Heman, Cindy Hochman ("100 Proof" Copyediting Services), Evie Ivy, Ami Kaye, Dean Kostos, Lissa Kiernan, Leslie Prosterman, Alison Ross, George Wallace, and Francine Witte, and to the members of *brevitas*, an online poetry community, and to Silya Kiese and members of her Art Students League workshop.

And additional thanks to Mary Ann, Susan, Naomi, Rosie, Rifka, Ange, Ann, Lois, and Phyllis for your continued presence in my life.

Grateful acknowledgment is made to my publisher Karen Kelsay and her staff for giving this manuscript such a beautiful home. I am honored.

Contents

Aesthetics	15
(blue) whisper	16
Border	17
Bridges	18
Cache	19
Companion	20
Couldn't Be More	21
Daydream as Moon	22
Dazzle and Shadow	23
Despite Magnificent Technique	24
The door to the endless	25
Early on	26
Encuentro	27
Ember	28
Faith	29
Fidelity	30
from my end of our sequence	33
The Girl Who Wanted to Go Fast	34
Green	35
Horse of a Different Color	36
How I Arrived Here	37
How This Hour's Raw Beauty Came to Enter	38
Without Leave	38
Inspiration	40
Intersect	41

Invention	42
Legerdemain, or Nostalgia, the Oldest Profession,	43
Pumps Her Prince of Magic, Recollection	43
Leisure	44
Losing Balance	45
Memory Riding Herd on My Heart	46
Messing with Mr. In-between	47
Mirrors Set in Sand	48
Not Quite Ready	49
Old House	50
Persephone	51
Private	52
Pursuit	53
Red State of Mind	54
Reverie	55
Sea Captain's Wife, Waiting	56
Seafarer's Hymn	57
She smiles, remembers	58
Small Sample	59
something we recall	60
Spring Sow	61
Stretched Around	62
The Success of Failure: A Fable in Show & Tell	63
Summoning Stones: Instructions and Narrations	64
Ten Ritual Views of Worry	66
Things to do with a Stone	70
Throwing Blind	71
Toward Maturity	72

Tremendous Idea	73
Truth is	74
Vector	75
Waiting to Find	76
Waving its Shaky	77
About the Author	79

… what I call 'my life,' it is not one life that I look back upon; I am not one person; I am many people.
—Virginia Woolf, *The Waves*

"It's nothing but" "what you've always known," "always been" "For you've always" "been being" "It's simple" "Simple."
—Alice Notley, *The Descent of Alette, Book Three*

Aesthetics

1.

Leer,
show teeth—

or budge that fat ass
click your dowdy heels;

pyrotechnics turn a mirror
to a moon.

Contemplation alters
illumination, sets

your somber gown
aglow.

2.

Amber plum
over the soul

a sum of words
to make
a jig or dirge. Instead

let moon return to gong.

(blue) whisper

I am connected to the (blue) whisper
and the answers always there
revealing themselves to me in phases
of years lived. I want to tie them
to the tunes, to the hungers, to the final
array shimmering with the finish
that finds me, however it finds me.

Border

Thinking out(side) that line
which then crosses itself
on the way back.

Snags.

Paused, I float, churning, tipped,
almost serene. Lake soul reflecting
sky bone.

Bridges

Immense traversed by a string of lights
imagined. Beneath, that-which-will-disperse-

on-scrutiny is lifting, lifting in order to peer in.
Until it succumbs to thought, or hour, or wind.

Building another bridge, this one dense,
sturdy, a study in suspension across space.

Y of center span=latest years.
How can we say our particular accumulation?

What can we say without it crumbling?

Cache

The cache of red to green clicked in the air   across the hall   until   time came it became time   to reveal   reveal
      oh!   everything   cracking on high, lost in low   the day adjusted taught me to open slowly to shine my pale
      through night's shadows through density into the *now* luring with layers of desire   into me and danced danced danced (spicy) dazzle down a hallway blazing   *someday* ever-changing even while sky-drenched hands turn it around

use the key to continue *now* turning   turning over
      brimming over

Erasure of my entire chapbook *Myself Taking Stage*

Companion

Doesn't swing me
along, doesn't wrap or warp;

doesn't take my hand,
then drop it.

Comes from around
the corner, then straight

into me, from me, a breath
of arrival, already here. Whispers

what pours from the soul
of the world, those parts

under stones, on the silver
side leaf shows to rain,

the rain itself.

Couldn't Be More

And I awaken into the seed's dream, into the bud's vision, to become a flower among flowers within a cluster of flowers just as wind lifts my petals off in several directions at once so that I find myself trembling across a southern province of China while tumbling over Mexico in a piñata's sweet release. My petals are taken between a child's fingers and smoothed across her cheek, then stuck to her nose just briefly, before I return to find I am my own clenched teeth in a mouth pursed in judgment. How to open out of it, and again, when my attempts do not lie content but are a winding road switchbacking up a mountain whose apex is lost in fog. And I use deep breath to shift ajar the door of my line of vision's fraction, and on entering, I do let go. Even a flower couldn't be more open.

Daydream as Moon

New: Daydream drinks whatever rises, has no memory to tell. She seals any sleeping shadow as she walks across a pointed surface in order to arrive.

Full: In your mouth, expanding like starch. All your tongues meet here: one in cheek, one in stone, the bleak one, one slippery as blade, and the one that spoke before you had words.

Waxing Crescent: Next time, daydream pulls your rain into a hard belly. Chipped glass is mistaken for lawn. Wild hair as if she is sorry. And those tears from her eyes—like melons in your hands.

First Quarter: You find your way back into her shadow. The ten worst memories arrange in descending order. Breakup, you think, and attach a string between doorknobs, find yourself singed by a searing scream.

Waxing Gibbous: Daydream slides scarves from your ears. The glamour in her eyes renders you obsolete. While you rotate, she snares you in every direction. Scarves wind 'round your head, drop on you as mist. You think you will see through mirrors with them. It is only another reflection.

Dazzle and Shadow

How do you know who you really used to be? The look back is a glance through cracked ice, reflection sending dazzle and shadow into your eyes. Any encounter is told with another voice in a timbre filled with wisp and tale. Beneath the ice, your lost Atlantis. You want to discover streets you missed, rooms you didn't find; want to punctuate prior hesitations with action instead of drear time. The girl you meet in the doorway might be you. Part of her waiting, part of her rushing ahead. Which part to ask—but look, there's yet another, trembling to be noticed. An abstract sensation branches from her tongue, takes the form of words, parts the cracks in ice.

Despite Magnificent Technique

Before we could relate the rest
of the story, it was over
because a new one had begun
and was telling itself
even as it, too, was about to sink
below its own beginning.

We who knew of the story
(were perhaps in the story)
tried to correct and auto-
correct the story's insistence
that it go where it wanted,
not where we hoped.

The door to the endless

is closing! Must run!
Will I? Won't I?
Something's going
quick enough to measure.

I rush to keep what's left
of what's leaving.

Early on

He made as stable morning glories / For the next to handle / Their regret
—Gertrude Stein, "Morning Glories"

Pulled back by the strings of your past—
see how they ripple, ripple & twine

until you realize they seize & squeeze
your accomplishments dry

with great regret, and you open,
open yourself to more, morning glory.

Encuentro

    after a painting by Remedios Varo

If blue it be/must be to lure
my eyes, to meet myself
as self, not girl, not separate
from now. Intact, we twirl
in cloth as swirl as sky
around, take form it gives
until my hollows fill
all my yearning years
within this shape of body.

Still I can't look away
and constantly peek back
into what held/still holds me
boxed & peering, in & out.
From here my soul
looks beyond and into sky.
And thus I go about
this hard business of living.

Ember

Just as we left it, smoking
as though fire partly quenched,

stark light obscuring red glow
while the ember strikes the bell.

Summers we danced on our lawn.
Barefoot, and beautiful, and bountiful.

I remain your eyes' pleasure
each dawn

not unlike a perennial in its time
over and over again.

Faith

A foggy glass globe
to carry like a small creature, beating

heart, body warmth. It disappears
into the daily, into the wars

and fires, into the weeping and floods.
I think it lost but then it unexpectedly

returns, surprising me
with its familiar persistence.

Fidelity

I hold them even
as they crumble. And all I can hold
is in my mouth and I say
some days they stumble out
like mistakes, then become
flags waving that turn into
indomitable dancers in realms
of fire, realms of ice,
and I, in them,
am nothing if not
myself.

Four Lessons Toward a Harvest of Voice

For a writer, voice is a problem that never lets you go
—A. Alvarez, The Writer's Voice

1. Listening

Gather your exquisite
listening skills and get deeper into,
into systems you might enter
beneath the natural ceiling—

There ...

your voice turns itself to listen
to itself listening back before word was
and only the first burst appeared and possibility
even what you couldn't make it.

2. Imitation

Is not just lesson. Is not just addition. Is not echo or simply unique.
And is. And is also: Cooked. Raised high above the head.
Dropped. Puked on in a binge. Returned and retuned.
Rotated until it's someone else.

Such mustering manages eventually.
Covered in butter cream one day, oiled and baked the next.
Rust revealed, and razor-slide bled. What's yours? How many
faces does it find before it finds its face?

3. Praxis

If the beautiful voice
is found sleeping
and you don't know how to waken her
with your petal pleas and tender tickles

do you wait until she rouses
herself, refreshed and freshened
from the loose dreams
she corralled with the silk lasso

or do you shake her awake,
ply her with caffeine,
question her intently
until she opens, spills…

4. Character

This is the character of voice.
Beneath the worrisome or winsome.
Beside the one that shows your stumbles and your triumphs.
Can you laugh like a cow? Do you peck the carrion of day?
The one in you insists that what you've tasted on the grass & sands
of summers, or overrun in autumns, has been enough.
You've had your share. People running through you
as though you were a field in spring.
The hammer falls and falls again; the ball will someday
strike the gong. The sky will shut into a narrow ledge, then fade.

What will your voice say when it's done?

from my end of our sequence

Sure took her time/   in appetite & squander,
in preponderance of aspects of   self/sky/creator/   & then:
consumed time seeking   (right hairdo, sexy response …)

Somehow, she always thought   she failed.

How to tell her, let her know
(as though she still exists)
she did okay.

The Girl Who Wanted to Go Fast

*... and the woman ...
ah, what the woman mostly notices
is how fast the girl went:*

She was a shy girl.

A patsy girl. A puddle from spot
shower waiting to be evaporated
and fall elsewhere. Or vaporize
into storm cloud.

A girl with chiaroscuro eyes.
Vector hands. A grabber. A gotcha.

Quicksilver even now, she quite
suddenly peeks out from the top
of time's long tube.

Waves at the woman, then
slips back between shadow and stone.

Green

after Jasper Johns, *Green Target*

Green hears me singing the blues and intervenes. She follows me into my dreams posing as curtain, as cycle, as movie star. She offers a bottle of herself, mint julep. Smitten, I am, and swamp haze. Until I come upon my fear of the snake in her. Of the lizard tail she can release and leave dangling in my grasp. Spiraling her concentric swirls around my wrist, I cogitate heartbeat and conception. In retrospect, she remains forever at my childhood side; protean, pliable, and perfectly plausible. When I break away to pursue my other love—blue—she reminds me I can simply add the yolk of sun to summon her return. Now if I can learn to omit fear from my life, I'll be young again, full of bull's-eye & whirligig.

Horse of a Different Color

Cold drawing endless circles in the day. While I, in urge to follow warmer routine, walk perimeters of slush. The hail comes down in pellets, stinging. There is no sign of color breaking through. So gray must make do ...

Craving: jonquil, butternut, lavender, azure, cornflower blue, and more ...

Winter is an island and it's lonely in its gray. Walker seeking sparkle of sun. My earmuffs green as hills, rising in spring's still-distant promise, somewhere a horse prancing in a field looking for a rider.

Thinking: cerulean, magenta, sparkle & glitter, glam of sun through leaves.

Where is the horse! To ride, ride along this gray day and into another color.

How I Arrived Here

When still young, I left
the safe home of myself
and ad/ventured into
a waiting, twisting thread

of freedom
and misinformation.
The original speck of entry
opened, became my new home,
where I found

I wasn't a total stranger
to myself. I still carried
my barriers, my fences, walls,
doors, battlements, weaponry,

armor, shields…
At first, they transported
easily as a cloud of feathers;
but over time they turned
to stone, to ice.

What else to do
but carve and chip
and make the most
of sun and rain.

How This Hour's Raw Beauty Came to Enter Without Leave

Relax said middle age when I woke up,
Dreams are for those who never heal. We healed.
   —Dabney Stuart, "Love Story"

1. Emptying

All the sand poured from my body.
My arms gave up their passion
and I more or less became
my next self. I wanted to (re)turn my face
into someone's crooked arm, be their muse,
forget an understanding of seasons
that seemed to leave me
nothing but the quartering of years.
How like an occasional eclipse I felt—so necessary
to shield your eyes.
But only if you look.

2. Refilling

Slipped from me, my body a stalk.
Sewn aspects lost their stitches.
Gravity of desire
peeled back, something warm inside
skimmed, became less of myself.
Had I known beforehand,
I still could not
have foreseen what emptying
leaves room for.

Inquiry

There is a growing worry about the impact of false information worldwide ...

—Heidi Taksdal Skjeseth, "All the president's lies: Media coverage of lies in the US and France"

Is this about the internal prism of interpretation? Or is it about the plastic that the prism has become. That once was glass. That once produced the rainbows on the walls, the sheets, across the face of a lover. Or is this about the lover? And everything that has been loved. And those things not loved, but happening. Or is this about what's happening? Things happening that must be stopped. Or is it about activism. And the long road ahead. The one no longer less traveled because we are so many of us. One of many roads. Leading to the future. Is this all about the future? Or must the past appear. Is this the past? It is. Without us doing what must be done, there may not be a future. That we recognize. Or want. Or want to pass on. To our children. This is about the children. All of them. Every single one. This is no lie.

Inspiration

In its prior existence, a promise, asleep.
As it began, it was noticed.
Unfolding its rag of insistence.
Displaying its flag of light.
As it shaped, it was spoken.
Effulgent. Replete.
In its seeking, it was attentive
as a parrot collecting
a crossing of echoes. Into
its very making, they chattered
until it faltered, then faded,
and finally undid. In its departure,
it breached, speechless inside itself.

Intersect

Which strings we clutch depends
on whose mouth first

fisted words from see;
or was it budded words,

and we clasp stems?
No difference—there's only

so much to grasp at once.
What's more, small holds *can* widen,

just push against—a corner!
opens into maw;

senses can't adjust immediately,
but lift beyond

their previous set. What breaks away
yaws close, and later we use

this-we-set-to-loosen-from
as an umbilical cord

that hauls us back. Here,
something is the same

we're almost sure,
but then, we're not.

Invention

An old story has acquired
many overcoats, some plush

beyond the threadbare of others.
Line them along

the tripwire row of years.
Make yourself yearn!

See how they change places,
how they change how

you think about your past.
See how they twist

and cling to each other
as though afraid

to wake you from their dream.
Notice when it is you choose

to wear a particular coat
and which one you always keep

directly against your skin,
and never remove.

Legerdemain, or Nostalgia, the Oldest Profession, Pumps Her Prince of Magic, Recollection

1.

Facing the river　　　　　sunrise,
my building,　　　　　　do you stand at your window
in your satin robe,　　　　where you showed me,
sipping coffee,　　　　　 sleep-rumpled, wondering...

2.

When you first opened　　your robe, you were naughty
as a magician　　　stuck fairly in my centered beast.
You let your eyes, urges　　drift
mirrors with both of us　　up front　　to explain how much
taking was giving　　　no story　 except us, why
we ever stopped ever is　 is　　　not　　*sleight of hand.*

Leisure

And to tell the truth I don't want to let go of the wrists of idleness, I don't want to sell my life for money.
—Mary Oliver, "Black Oaks"

The same edge luring me forward
to more, not the same. The same

credenza puckered and overflowing
with knowing not owned, but—this is new—

promising to be known in the sun's entering
the brow, lids of night laddering the dream,

bells ringing in the swill of self-selected occupation.
This kind of attitude is vacation, this vacation my kind—

endless and changing. I get to drive. Get to swim.
Contemplate arrival at the chant, enchanted.

Losing Balance

I swagger away from my latest birthday, days before.
It's an act of rebellion, balance, and a mismanaged iliac.
All of which visit me daily in an attaché case designed
to look like a portal. Inside, my pills, which remind me
of my increasing fragilities: difficulty navigating windy
corners or how direct engagement in the din of crowded
spaces is becoming impossible. A sorrow that in dream
has settled deep into my chest leaves an impression
on waking. I stagger into day with the aid of caffeine.

But it's the morning news that knocks me over.

Memory Riding Herd on My Heart

Elaborately coiled
       & almost cruel

from a distance that cannot
       cannot be

touched, but flavors
       & flashes

urge-splashed
       desire

twisted in the deep
       solvent of longing

almost shy
       as it pinions itself

stitched & pining
       behaving as though

I am its guest
       and not its host.

Messing with Mr. In-between

Don't mess with Mr. In-between
—Johnny Mercer, "Accentuate the Positive"

> *In between pendulum*
> *& pit, archive & chronicle,*
> *labyrinth & jive...*

was skin- &
dabble-fest. Feast of the night
undoing the diet. Until

string with drama
backed against itself. I was purely
hoping for, I mean *hoping*

the way some might
mean *praying*. Yes, I wanted
that much.

My arms turned tentacles
grasping extant
& extinct.

> *In between parapet & gargoyle,*
> *lodestar & lodestone, blood*
> *clot & ink...*

Mirrors Set in Sand

    after *Les plages d'Agnès*

Reflected in mirrors set in sand, she sees
someone she recognizes.   Superimposed.
Over herself, herself.   She asks
the past.   To leave her   here
and to not   replay
everything/everyone   gone. Such
beautiful people,   like she too was
so young until such time
as their youth became   an illusion
of self, a dream.   In a mirror you can   stand before
who you were.   If you're still
enough   you may see   who's left.

Not Quite Ready

I aged into an overripe
then into a rough sketch
then into a dotted-swiss dirndl
and finally into this hewn
tiny house, all windows looking out
at skies of infinite continuation
I'm not quite ready to step into
but have my walking sandals
by the door where I can see
my first childhood
already coming toward me.

Old House

The truth is a reflection
in the mirror in the hallway
in the old house. But, which old house—
the one that's fallen
or the one that never got built?

Persephone

Pulling the hole over my head and covering the eyes. The mouth. The ears. The heart. Nightfall underground is no morning. It is ever. Descend. Once there, arrived, a new view. Special shades poured from shadow. Pert canopies and awnings. Specter forms hovering close. Tumble again. I am fallen in love. My large frets shrink. My climbing quests reside in the near-at-hand. Robed and deft-sided, he sparks me with his un-rove attentions. Above, the trees are dead. The mountainous night holds thrall. He uncovers my heart. One swift tug I'm bare. Noticing a newer cleft, cleaving where we left off, he wildly ruffles, then smooths. Over and over, we are beside, in and out. Each other a part. Upstairs is winter, seasoned to blow around, swig and swirl detritus. Below, in our mountain beneath, his reign I beg forgiveness for later; now there is no reason that can cajole me not to. Though I am sorry, I am more not. I am story. I am stalk, bud, flower, fruit—cycle arrive after my pleasures.

Private

Clinks in the drawer with the cutlery.
Can cut. Or dish it out, leaving
you too full

or too empty. Softened over time,
a stinky, melted cheese the maggots
swirl upon

and you stay out of that room, and you,
without full awareness,
use martial arts

to keep it away. As though it's labeled
Private and not yours at all,
and even if it is,

you won't lend yourself a hand
to lift it, even to just
have a peek.

Pursuit

And finally, to that wonderfully sweet glory I sometimes encounter when I forget that I am singing, and, at last, this singer gets to become the song.

—Alan Neuberg, "Bridging Secular and Spiritual Approaches to Neurotic Misery and Everyday Unhappiness"

Many times I've been   so close,
sliding somewhere,
perhaps even toward home
when I suddenly think…
—and it's gone…

Nooked in a cranny, pole vaulter, loose leaver,
looser, flitting, ill-conceived
mountain of trouble at the back door.
I've preened and pranced, observed and stashed,
burnt offerings,
gnashed
my dizzy hands busying myself completely
while the sun rose and set.

Yet, many times I've been   so close, *closer,*
day listing toward dog,   an unmoored sentence
rises in a puddle: who why what when—answers
the world in reflection, I lean over—

                so close, closer—*that close,*
inside actually, peering out the same eyes.

Red State of Mind

Wish I could stay my medallion arguments. Catch your *never mind* until it raises onto its elbows. There I'd slip under your heightened, twine my tape, split half to quarter and remain past longer. I'm forever just about to, spacing hesitation into bottled lines upon the window ledge, light flowing through in seams. Remembered association trying to pretend another song, another singer. Afterglow sits pretty posture, braiding her hair, long out the window. She'll climb down some night, run the seeded field.

Reverie

Nothing to touch, no matter. The blessing we hope for in memory wanders in a wilderness. Unspoiled by ravage. Free of disappointment. Spending time appearing in unexpected places—transit platforms, lunchtime streets, a theater restroom line. The way light catches someone else's curve, the note a voice sounds on first leaving the throat to speak. The way our eyes and ears, without our suspecting, are ever seeking to see again someone dearly loved who's gone.

Sea Captain's Wife, Waiting

I took to eating dried figs while remembering
slick sweat between my breasts
when we made love.

There is always
having and losing,
losing and having—
continuous, slapping.
At first, the losing gave an edge
to having

until it ebbed something away from me,
and even while I am having,
I'm remembering only loss
to come.

Seafarer's Hymn

I cannot make out what I see
In the dark I enter.
   —Owl Woman, "In the Dark I Enter"

O cold light lunge
plunge from dark above
open   moon light
so it does not press me so.
hips can tease me
as you
sash upon these waters
as you   pull me
touch me

far as my eye can reach;
through dark below   cool
before me the dark before me
No lover's lips   no insistent
ease, appease me now as you
lie upon, fall upon,
a path that I can follow
with your more-than-human pull,
with your perfect human touch.

After Cædmon's "Hymn" and "The Seafarer" *(*from the "Exeter Book" and from Pound*)* and William Carlos Williams, *thus moonlight is the perfect human touch.* Also, Gloria Ortiz-Hernández's painting *Crossing Aided By a Pillar of Light.*

She smiles, remembers

He buys her
a paper fan

that opens, full moon
with dragon and ripe

plums. The silent brush of him
exactly as imagined.

Already folded back,
new moon.

Small Sample

I'm a small sample. Of a micro part. Of less.
Yet within is an always. Is an all.
I must remember the universe. The proportion.
That I am portion. Have a portion. Use it.

I call it to me & call it 'mine.'
{What} have you called yours?
Sometimes I swear I can almost reach through
and stand where all the dimensions

overlap. And there I am, riding my scooter, my bike,
driving the car down the highway to the beach.
A baby, my baby, latches onto me. Later,
I let her go. She goes. This is a small sample

of my small sample. Entirely my own and
fused to the continuum. Much like you.
Like yours. Together, we make what all this is.
We need to offer each other our hands.

something we recall

… and the whole
day spins its tales. And the hours are brisk
and efficient. What we get is what we see.
Ever-after recedes back to something we recall
and call after.

Spring Sow

Dearest Now,
sweet
rows of pea seeds
planted near the trellis.

Dear Ninth-grade Biology,
nudging today away.
You were sweet-pea
genetics, dominant eyes.

Dearest Boy and Girl,
sharing
frog &
scalpel.

Dear Yesterday,
you shuttle train, you huckster,
luring me back
& back.

Stretched Around

I remember myself
opening to receive another time waving at the threshold, quick to understand waiting might be a glimpse. Calmness settled me until my head filled the ever-changing, amazing, lovely *next*. I opened my pale, waited through density with ease, shine, and chrome. I could carry my voice stretched around flame,

stretched around my daily, aflame with shine and chrome. I opened my pale to attach stars until my head filled with searching to find moon fragments quivering upon water, answers ever-changing. I love the girl I used to be, wild, rummaging to understand meaning, determination in my arms. Holding all reflected,
I remember myself.

Erasure forward and backward of my chapbook *Myself Taking Stage*

The Success of Failure: A Fable in Show & Tell

after reading "Five Marks of Oft-Rejected Poems," by Michael Mlekoday

1. It was early morning and I was already boring

2. into my own buoyant spring, which was stuck to the top of an acrylic ceiling like a static-y balloon, crimson as the lips of the Ouroboros eating her tail

3. while attempting to transcend the (meta)physics of Plexiglas.*

4. Bumping into my drill bit, it burst and propelled, not up and away, but spinning down to the floor.

5. O red gasp of polychloroprene. Rejected heap. Squalid and flat. Unworthy. Un-redemptive. Lacking allure.

> 5a. *Postscript*—Later, someone (the child?) came across it, stretched it across fingers, then tongued it, then waved it around. Carried in her pocket (next to her heart), it was eventually washed with the laundry, then collaged onto a picture of sky…

---

* While Plexiglas might, metaphorically, bring to mind the glass ceiling that keeps women and others from rising to the top ranks of the corporate world, the ceiling might also be Lucite, which could connote, again metaphorically, lucidity/lucidness. In either case, the clear transparency permits seeing what's beyond confines—in this case, to the outside, where the balloon's fervent wish is to become part of the sky.

Summoning Stones: Instructions and Narrations

I will search the reality of you...
   —Isamu Noguchi

Instructions

Within a dish, they overlap and sleep. Wake them and lay them in a circle. Lay them in a line. Pass them from hand to hand. Touch them to your most pallid parts. Lick them. Call them. Call them in tongues. Set them in the sun. Set them in bowls of water. Summon them to repeat what they first spoke to you that made you pick them up.

Narrations

Notice the brown eye on my edge, sculpted by a break. Whoever danced on me did so outside the circle. Lonely, and no real stone, I am a Druid yawn. My heat fills a portion of your palm with memory, tongued and light. I slept under the moon, entered by distances. Every kind of time poured into me. I lead you to the code built upon the plain.
   Broken-walkway stone, Salisbury Plain, near Stonehenge

Twin singers. Pillars of salt. What memory heard during the last cycle when you called the storms by rubbing us together. Now we make you thirst. As we grow, we fill with bruises. If you drop us, we could bore a single, silent hole. Always return to our voice, as though we are a ladder. What we cannot teach you is too new.
   Crystal twins bought from a street vendor, East Village

Whoever touches my fish lips with their mouth will never underestimate both sides of a heart. Taste the salt I inherited. Use me to outline. Press me until the world seems flat. Seize my scales and use me under night. You hope you will never lose me, for you feel nearly perfect as I run smoothly over your skin.
   Black heart-shaped stone, Bar Harbor

I am an egg designed in creation. What can you do with me except hold me on my back. Inside, I contain the sound of the beginning. Toss me. I will infer what you wonder. Read my fine lines on coarse grain, as though you use wind as a finger to stir sand and water into design. Like you, I am only now.
   White oval stone with brown markings, Dead Sea

Ten Ritual Views of Worry

Worry is not preparation
    —T-shirt proverb

i.

Your body had been empty
and is suddenly full
of itself again!

ii.

—fill crevices, holes, all your curves;
inundate, speculate, obfuscate
the downs between your ridges.
Even into skin folds, the most delicate.

iii.

—that stooped shoulder, the slight
twitch near your eye. You're getting
ready for a big one. Are you ready?
Have you ordered the cake?
Made the dress? It fits
over worry's shape like weather.

iv.

What color is it, anyway?

v.

A raw taste?
A textured aroma?
A breeziness—
Brash. Brass. Two-lunged instrument.

vi.

When it lands, you're awake.
That is what waking is. Today
you place it in a different place
than yesterday. Perhaps someplace
new, someplace not previously touched.
Let's see if you fling it about, or yourself.

vii.

Worry is best examined
in its absence. Then you can see
what it is you are when it is out for its walk.
It has gone for a loaf of bread and jug of wine—
worry likes to celebrate all your occasions,
even the ones you've forgotten.
When it arrives back home, it claims
your stomach, intestines, lungs, bladder, neck,
rectum, sinuses, and the edge of your tongue.

viii.

Don't say "I worry." Say instead "it worries."
Then pluck it out by any means available.
Bunch it into a wad and put it outside your ribs.
Use a forklift to suspend it
above your reclined body.
Entice it to attach to temporary tasks
(clean the toilet, throw out the trash, pick up
worn socks from under the couch).

ix.

terrorists might come   bomb might explode
boss might see   child might get lost
child might take drugs   mother is dying
didn't study for the test   can't get the ball
into the basket   I'm flat   where's my
assignment?   will he/she call?   I've gained
15 pounds   nothing to wear   house a mess
I'm spending money   I'm not as good as
I'm getting old   I'm losing my looks
I'll get sick   he'll/she'll leave me
I'll get hurt   I'll run out of money
a dangerous storm is on the way!

x.

Because it has a shimmer that hovers over everything, you take it for party wrap, place it on a small (the blue one) mirror on the shelf you can see from your bed. Looking at it from a downward angle, well … you have your visual infinity. What fun! You can run amok inside, always believing you'll find the one true way out. Meanwhile, you keep busy appearing as though you have purpose.

Things to do with a Stone

- Toss it into (air/water/hole/basin).
- Toss it off (cliff/roof/branch).
- Imagine what it tells (time/memory/formation/journey) and what it doesn't (/).
- Cradle it against your (lips/forehead/hips/left breast).
- Lick it ((after a swish/a dip) in (creek/stream/river/sea/birdbath in the middle of the garden)).
- Notice variations of (surface/color/symmetry).
- Refrain from preaching to it. (Don't mention it's hard to swallow or that it's a burden to carry or push up a hill.)
- Heed its roll. Forward or back.
- Consider gravity's pull when picking it up.
- Name it with the name you call yourself in sleep.
- Leave it on the headstones of ones loved best. Make it promise to get the message to them that you've visited. In case they weren't looking when you came.
- Respect it. No matter your age, it's older than you.
- When you finally ask about the wars it's seen, whisper the question. It may have been trampled upon. A dead body may have pressed against it, causing a dark stain. It may have been hurled by hand or placed in a sling and shot. Or it may have simply watched, stunned & helpless. As you/I do on the screens in our homes and restaurants.

Throwing Blind

In the discursive,
an ocean of tides
under moon's pull.

Throwing blind into dark
toward a precipitous
future.

Change taking
almost everything
taken for granted

Toward Maturity

Along the lakeside route,
sunrise about to set sail
across a smooth question—

On the third try, what was reached
taught more than failure. Which spoke
in the mother tongue, ripened

with age.

Tremendous Idea

Be wild, that is how to clear the river
—Clarissa Pinkola Estés, *Women Who Run with the Wolves*

Then a tremendous idea flashes its backside
at you in the dark. You hear its raspberry tongue
sound a dare. If you fall into dream, you'll lose
the scent, lose the string you're conscientiously
following over scree that is under your feet.
You feel the grip of sleep pulling you
hard, down into a familiar garden
where the tremendous idea is praying for you,
praying you find it on every sheet, divining
a redemption, dancing under a floodlight
of rain, willing itself to spin out of control
onto the floor of your four-chambered beat.
Secrets pass hands there, and ideas are wild.

Truth is

I lied about what I wanted. Instead I wrote a thank-you note for what I got. When I tricked myself once too often, I tripped myself. And on up the stairs. To see the stars. There he kissed me. That was not a lie. Or not a lie I knew as a lie. This lasted a long time. Years, in fact. That's a lie. I lied to myself to make it last. At last, it broke. Nothing ran out. I had been empty. Even the lies were gone. I love here now. I still lie to myself but, truth is, I don't know it.

Vector

Remember the small approach allowed
into the vector of self-awareness

or how the lady slipper in the field stole
your attention from the blade

carried between your teeth. Did you have
hands yet that could pat a broken

heart worn to the quick from want?
How much dutiful daughter escaped

in your trenchant sighs, how much
serenity was caught on the escarpment

between childhood and the rest?
When did you become this other

who forgets the folding of bodies
into knots meant to hold forever

and ruminates instead in the landscape
of letting go, at the abutment of no regret.

Waiting to Find

1.

The girl was waiting to find something she didn't know what.
The wait takes up as much space as a giant machine.
The girl climbs the machine hoping to reach the top.
She believes the view will be endless.
The top of the machine is flat and dusty. Reclining on her back,
a ceiling is before her eyes.
How would you describe the electricity of anticipation?
The letting go of expectation.
The renewal of a false start. And again.

2.

Arrival is a position. It can be dark or light. Heavy or weightless.
Arrival holds the girl as the girl presents herself.
The girl is lost to the ensuing years.

3.

What the woman recalls—or thinks she recalls—
is like a machine with numerous folded footholds
that can each be activated with a lever to start
the whole recall from different angles.
The woman is researching how many angles memory has.
While waiting to find out, she slips further and further away from
the girl.

Waving its Shaky

There—that one. Waving its shaky.
Rolling its perky, stroking its regular size.
Extolling an unsaid, an undone, a redone, a hash
of a batch, a piece of this thought and that, lackadaisical
and smashing, downy and sequined, a mosaic
from beach glass rubbed smooth by time.
It can shimmer all it wants. Or simmer (it's summer!)
or hide in a tank. Soft cola edges already dissolving.
Hole in the middle spreading to fingers. Lifting the sheer
weight of the hour. And promising, promising
it will reveal in a singular shine.

About the Author

Karen Neuberg is the author of the poetry chapbooks *Detailed Still* (Poets Wear Prada, 2009), *Myself Taking Stage* (Finishing Line Press, 2014), and *the elephants are asking* (Glass Lyre Press, 2018). Her poetry and collages have appeared in numerous publications, including *805 Literary and Arts Journal, BOXCAR Poetry Review, Really System, S/TICK,* and *Verse Daily*. She is a multiple Pushcart and Best of the Net nominee, holds an MFA from The New School, is associate editor of the online journal *First Literary Review-East,* and lives in Brooklyn, New York.

www.ingramcontent.com/pod-product-compliance
Lightning Source LLC
Chambersburg PA
CBHW021024090426
42738CB00007B/890